We Like

BITCH

Brilliant Swear Word To Color

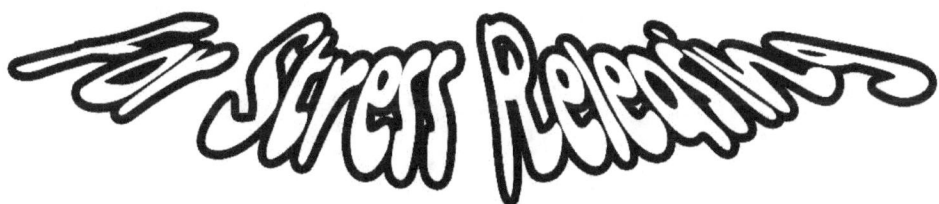

For Stress Releasing

Bear Smit Kibet

Happy Coloring!

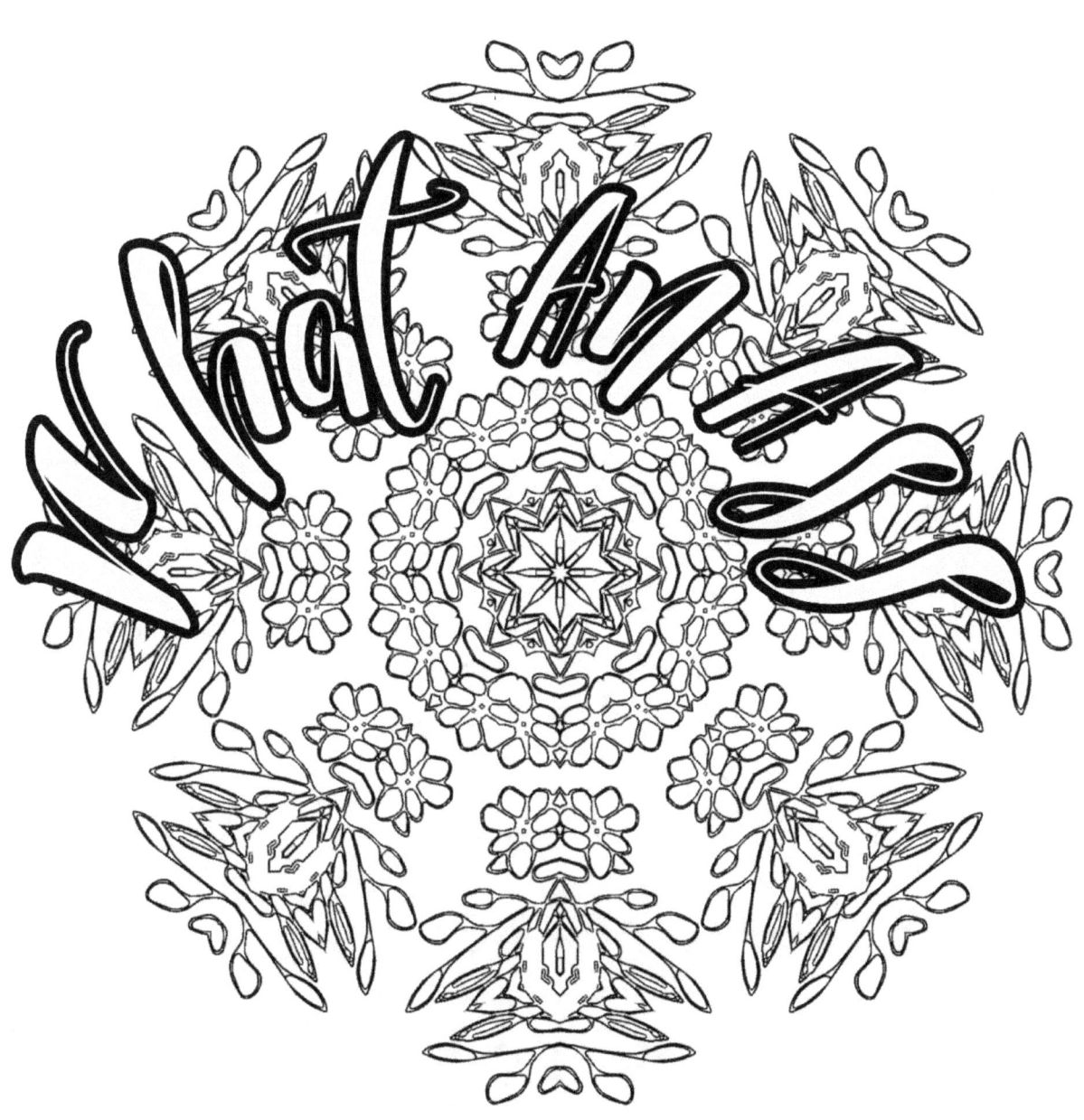

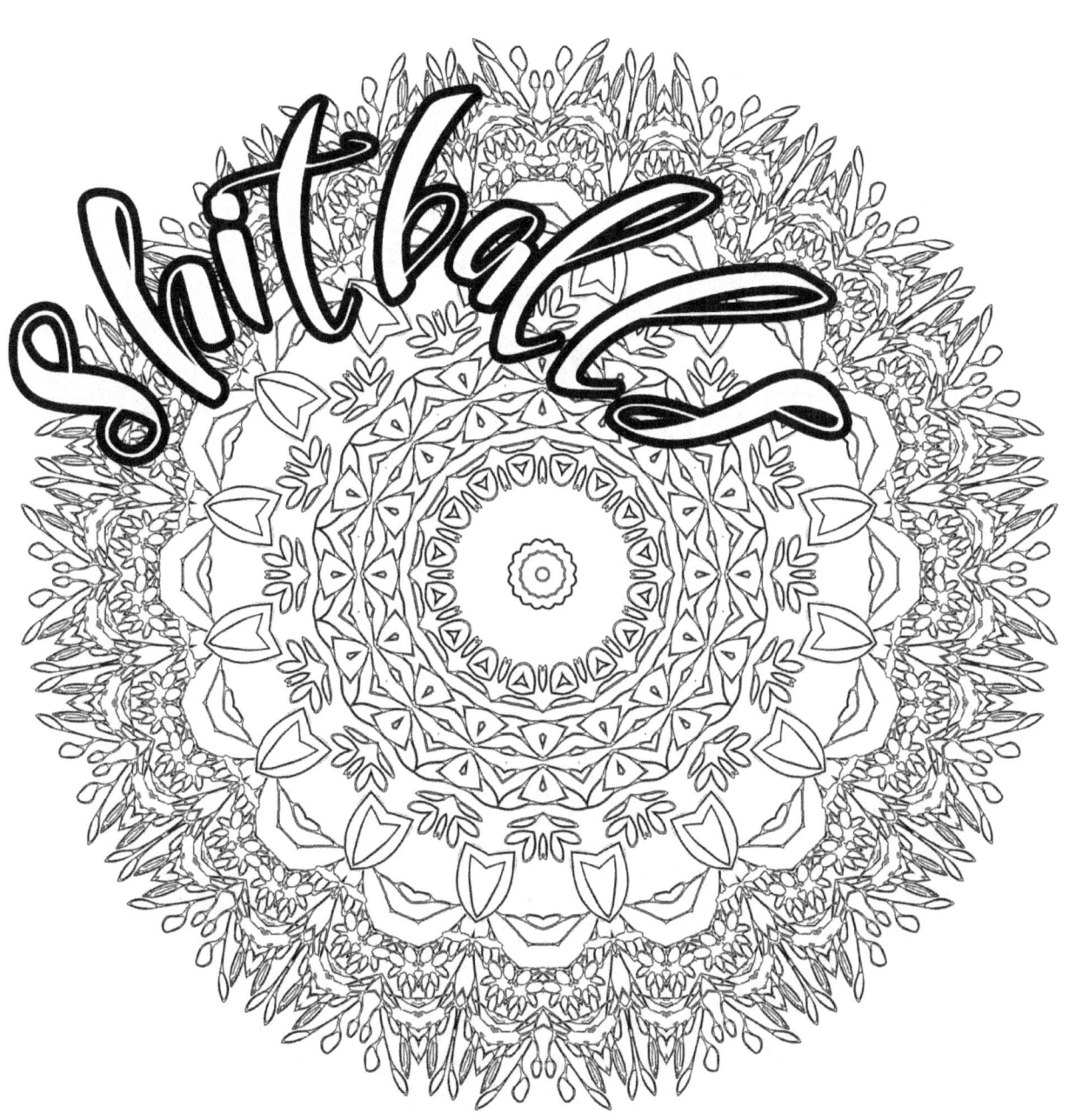

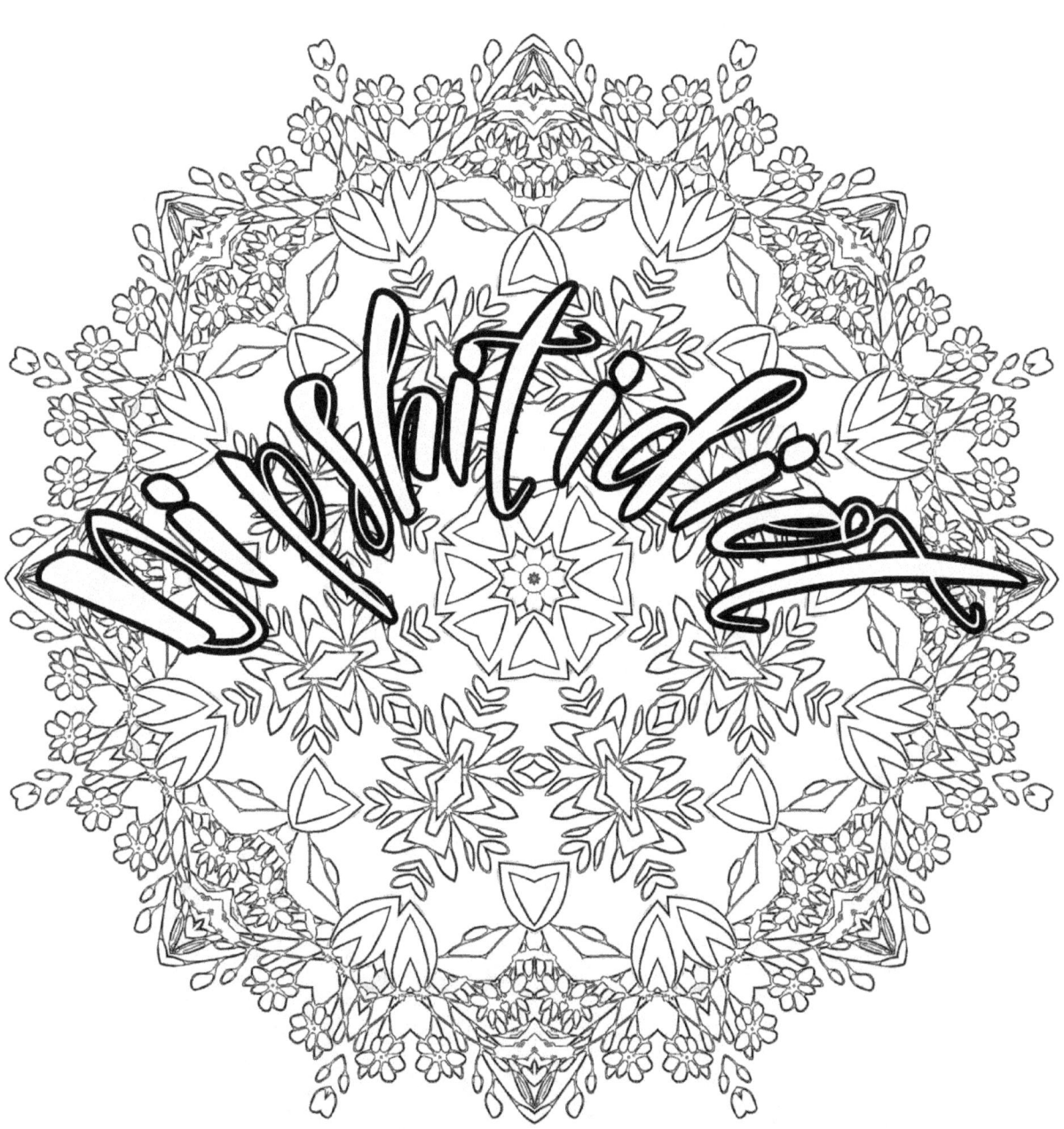

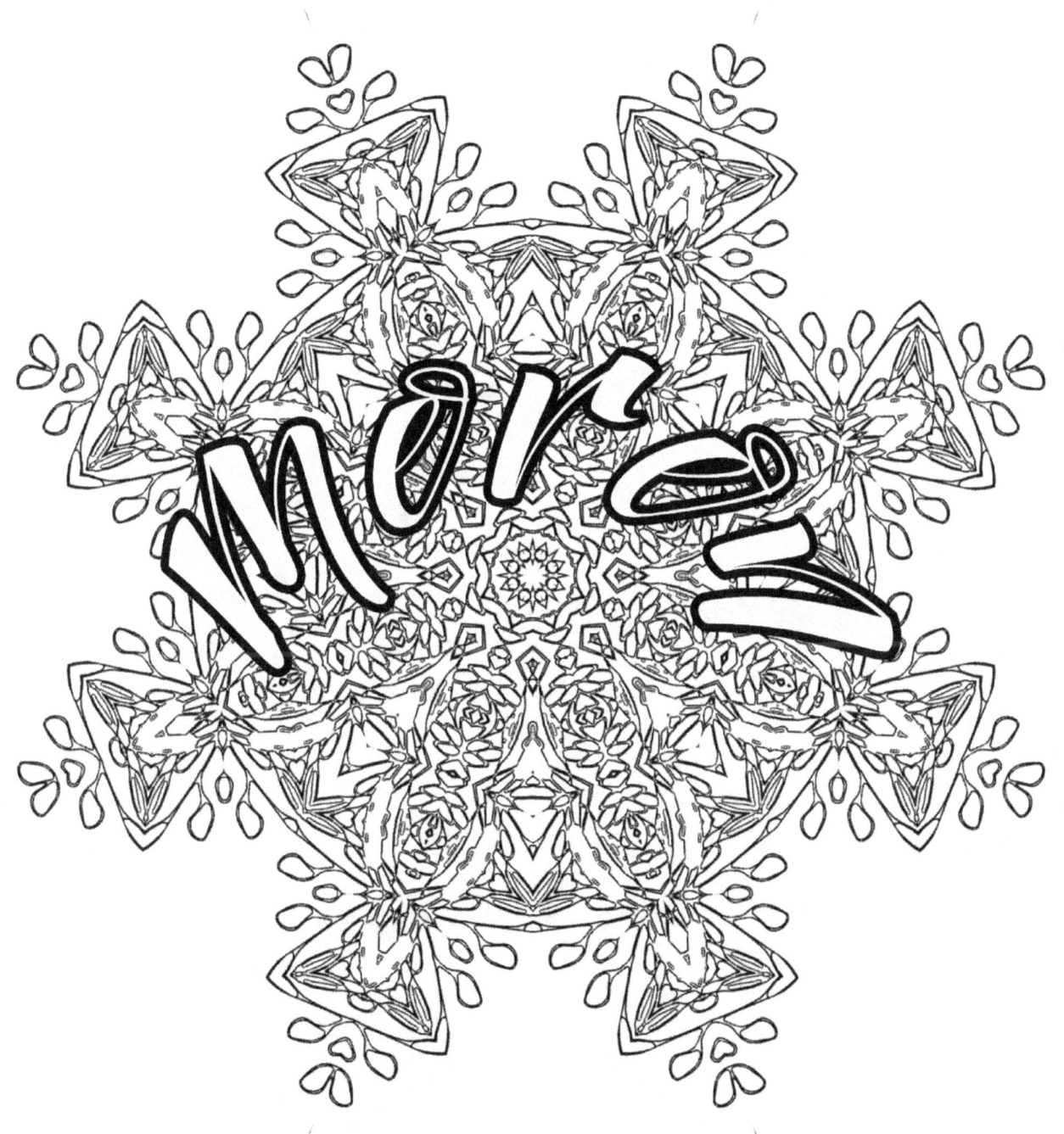

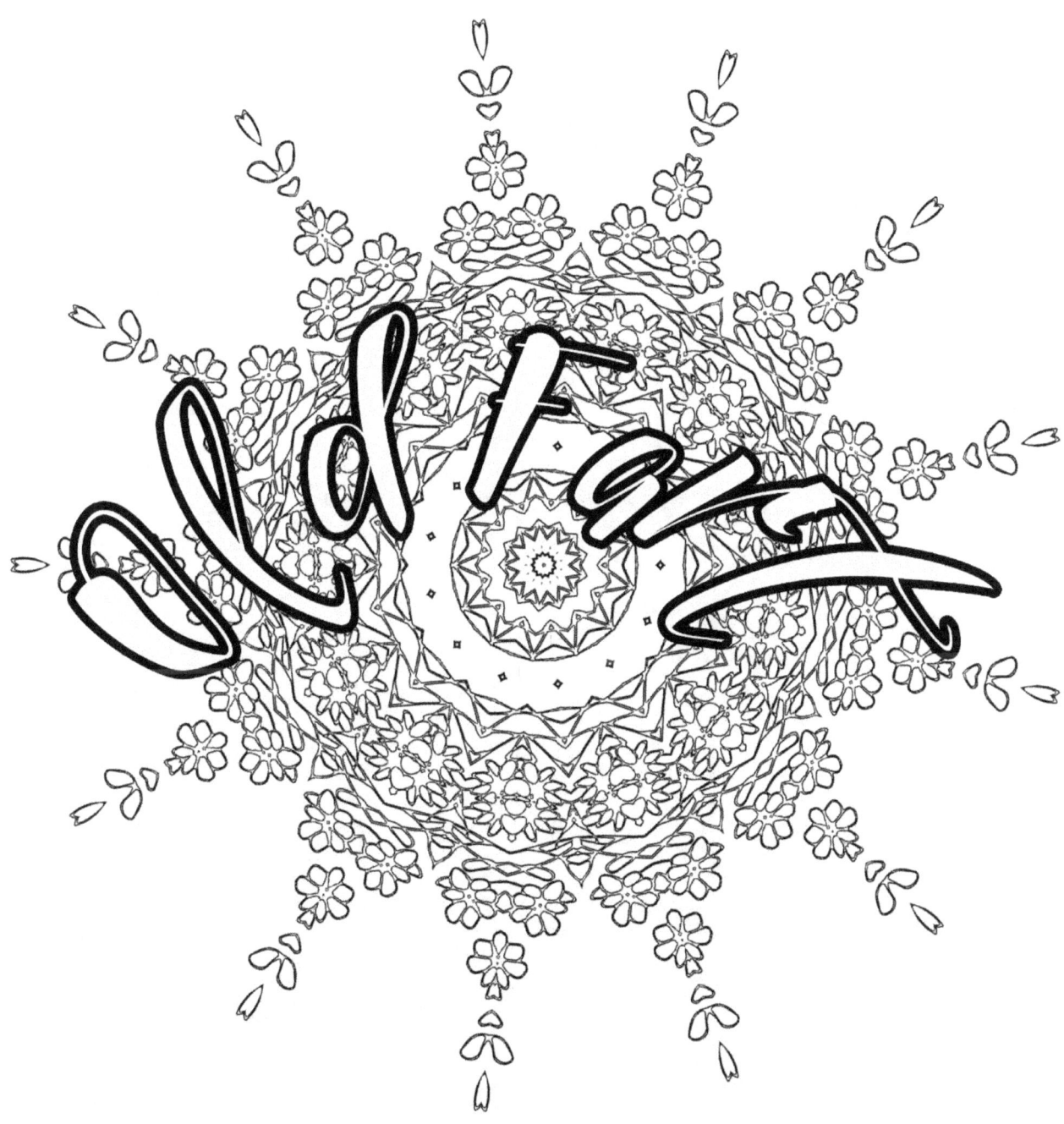

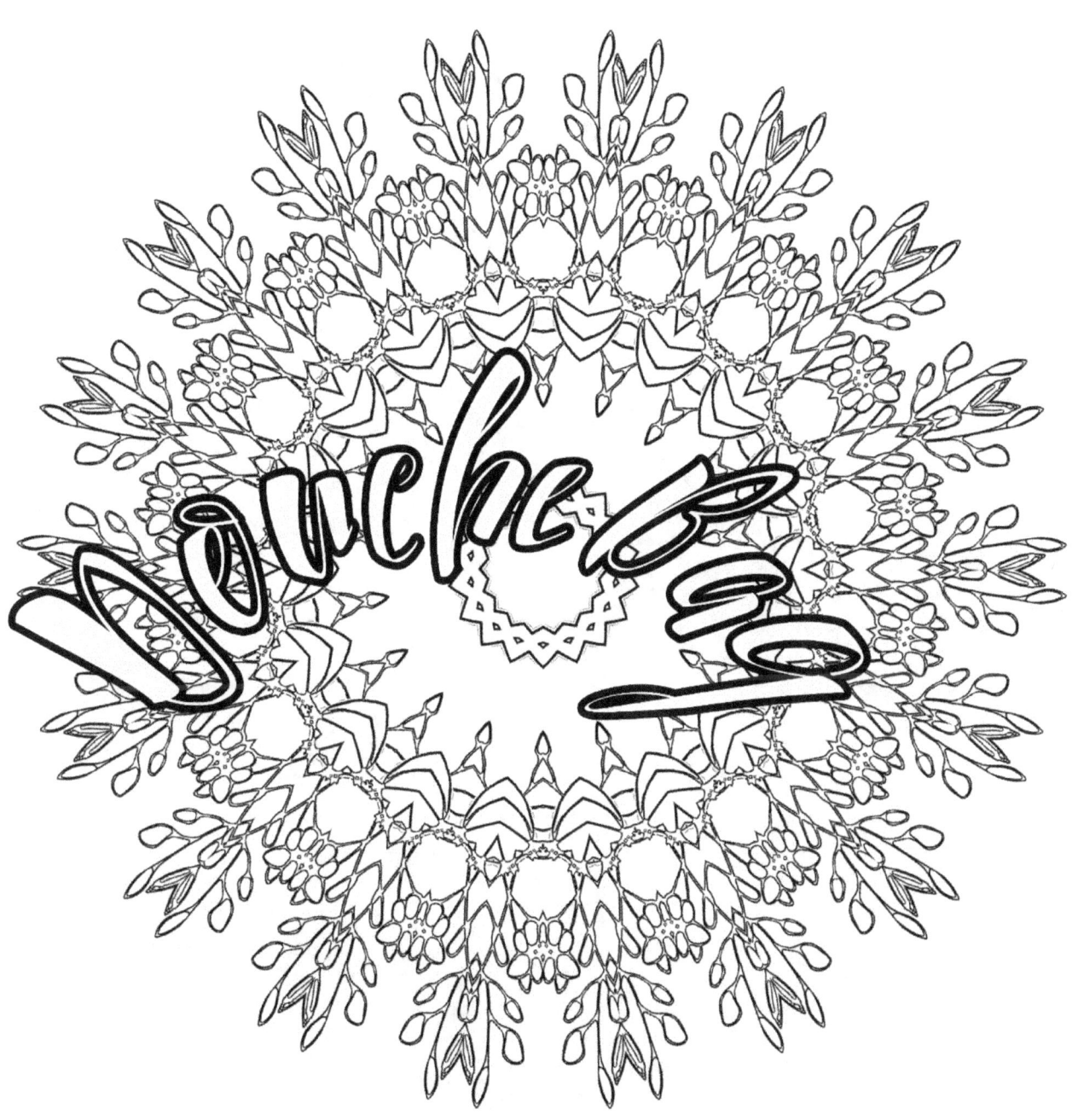

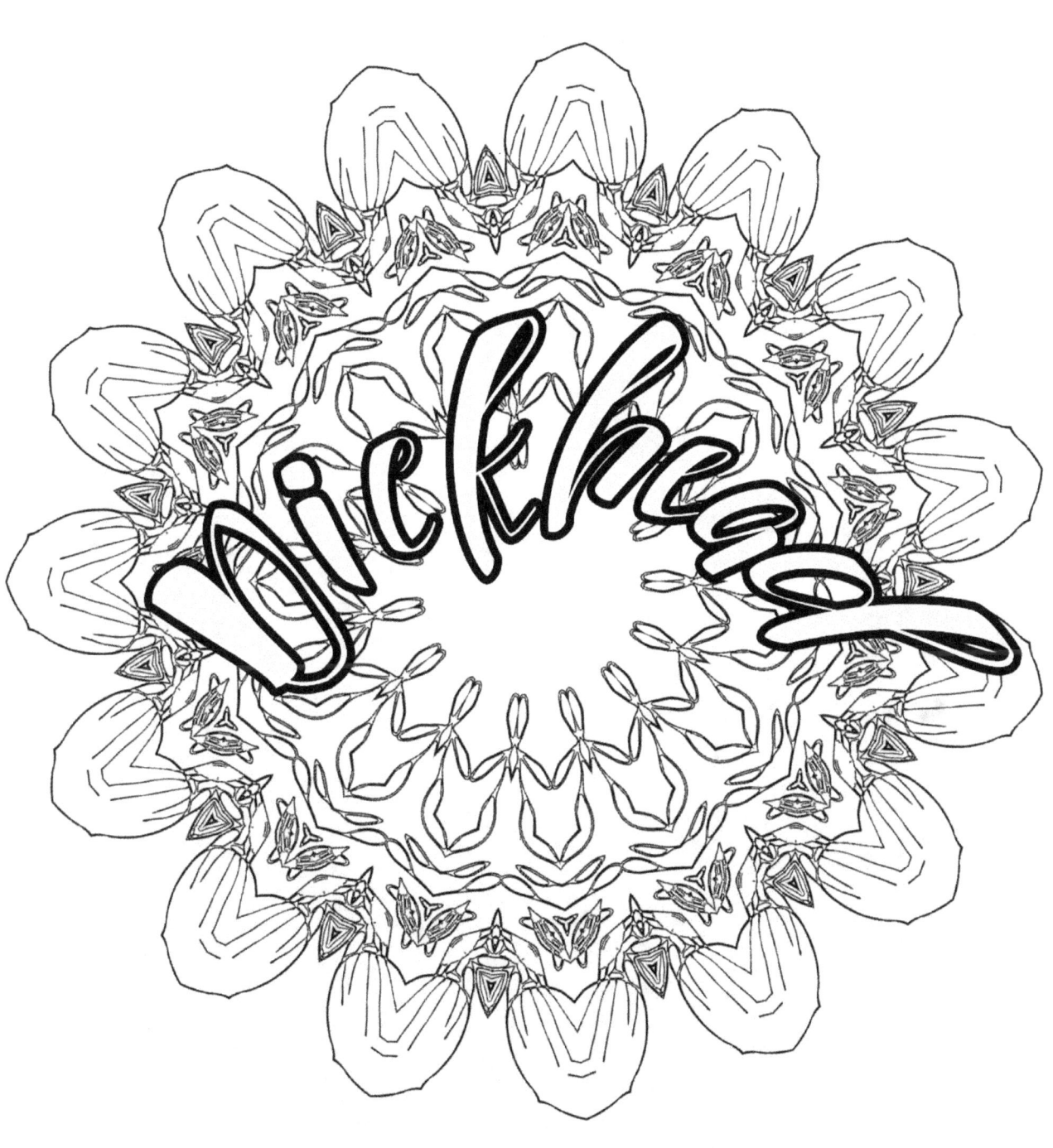

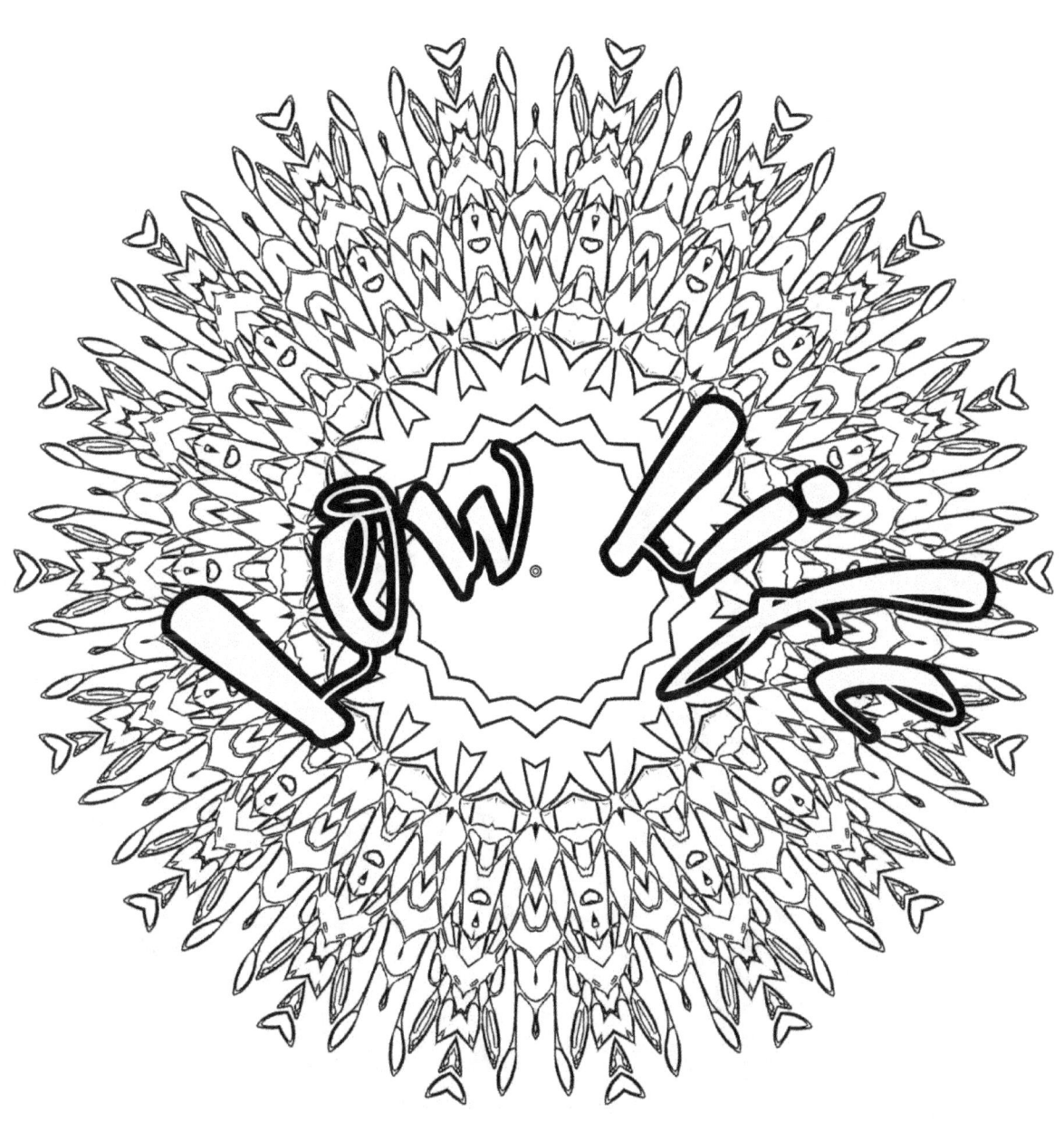

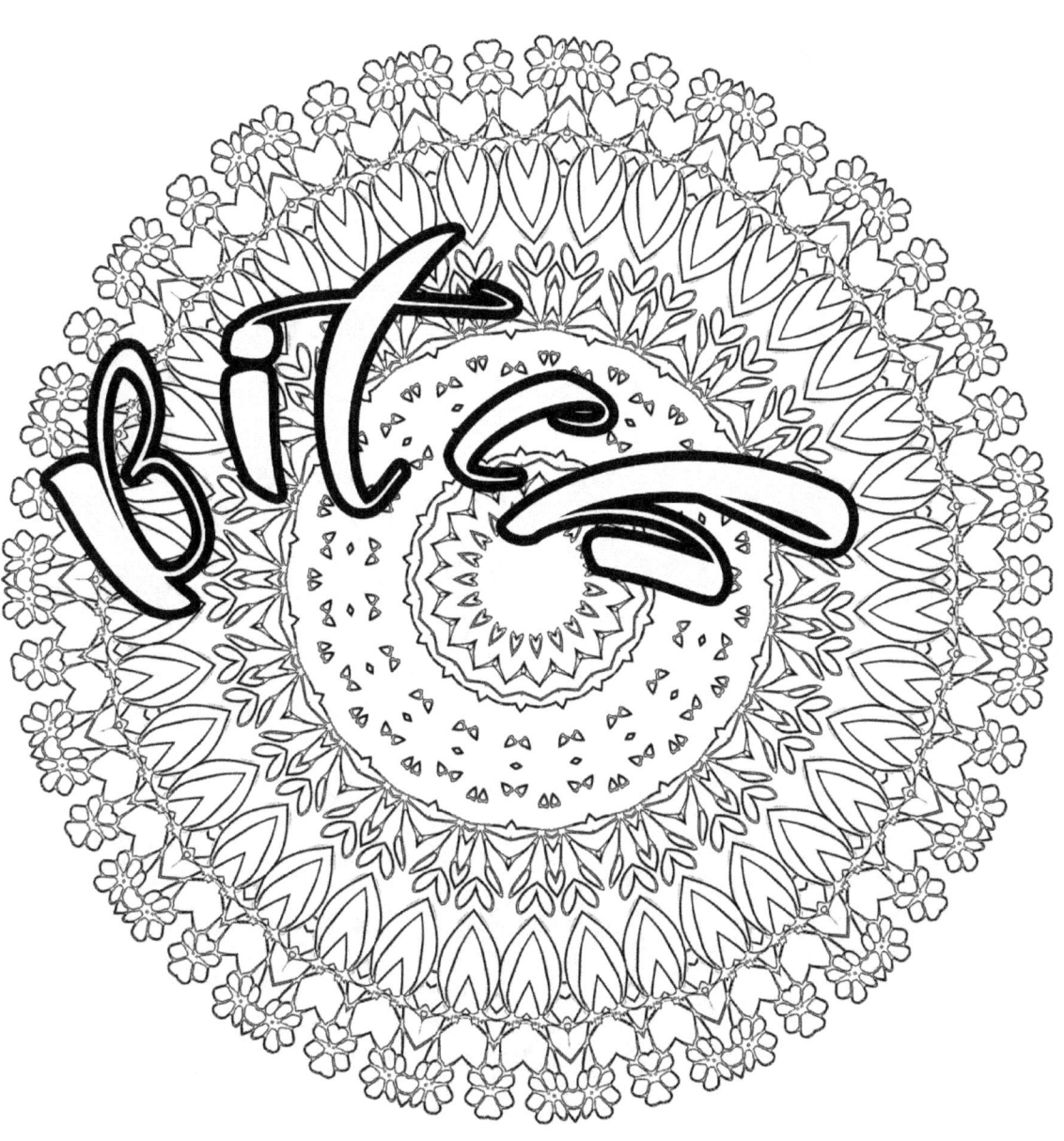

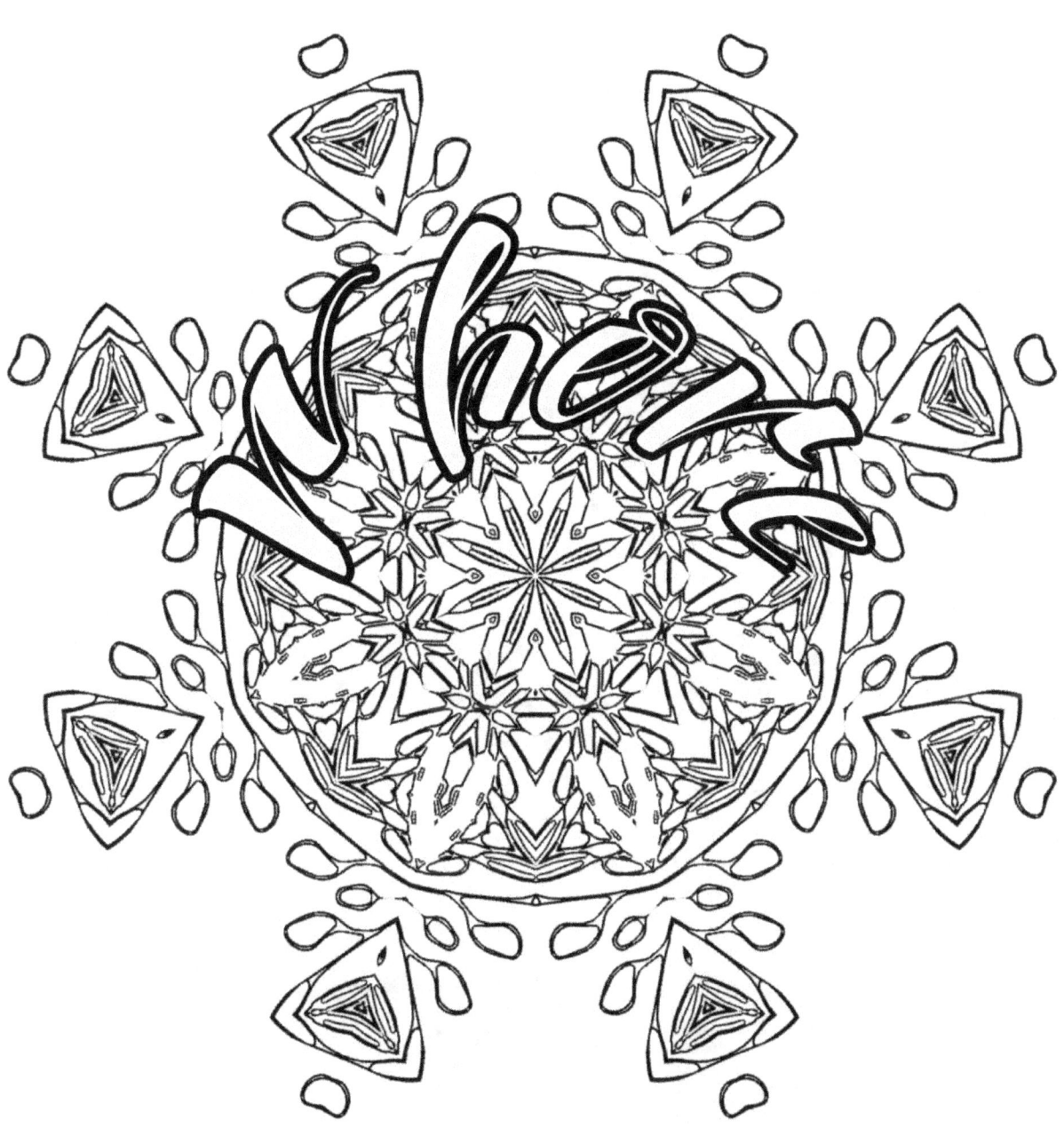

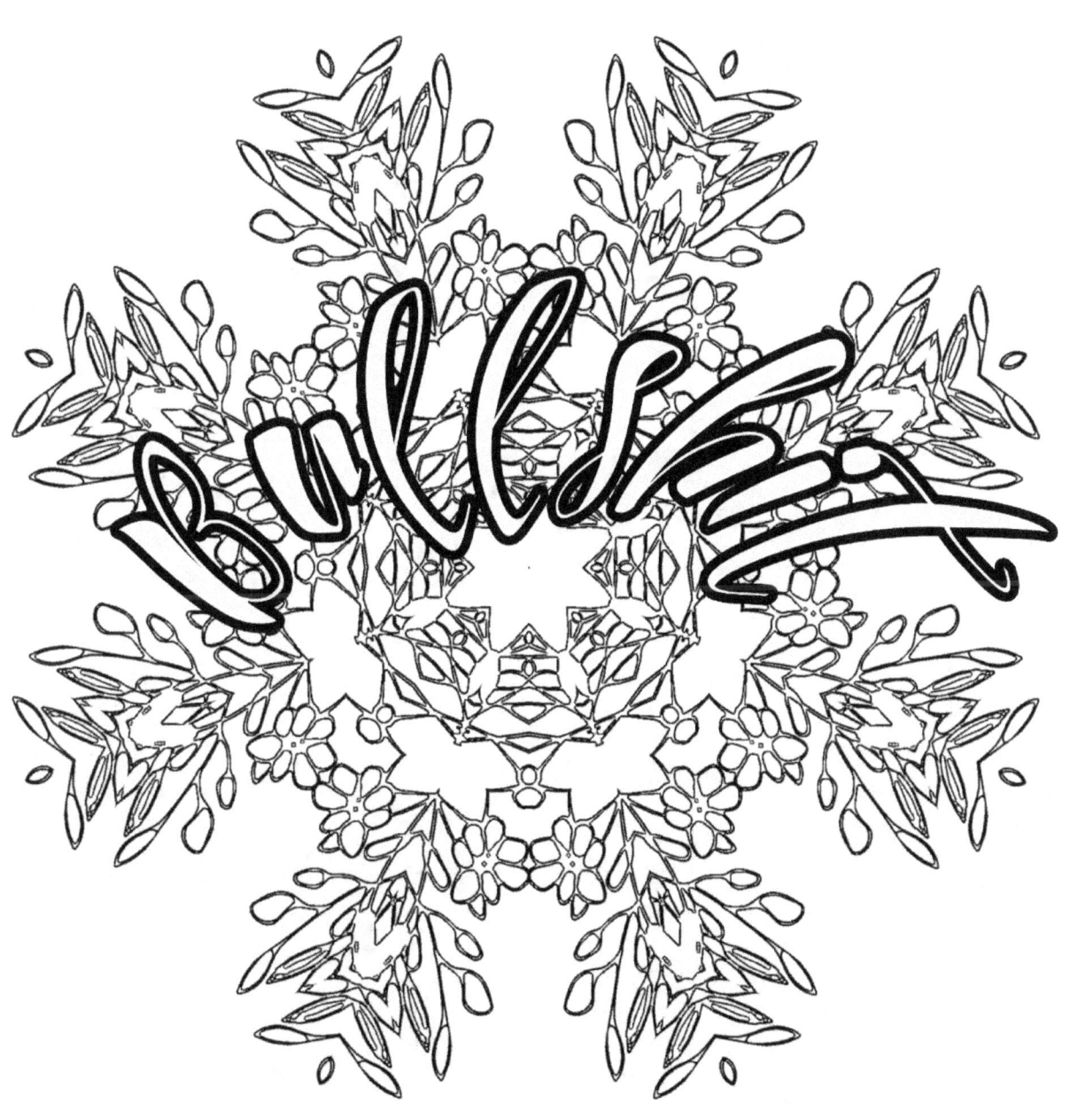

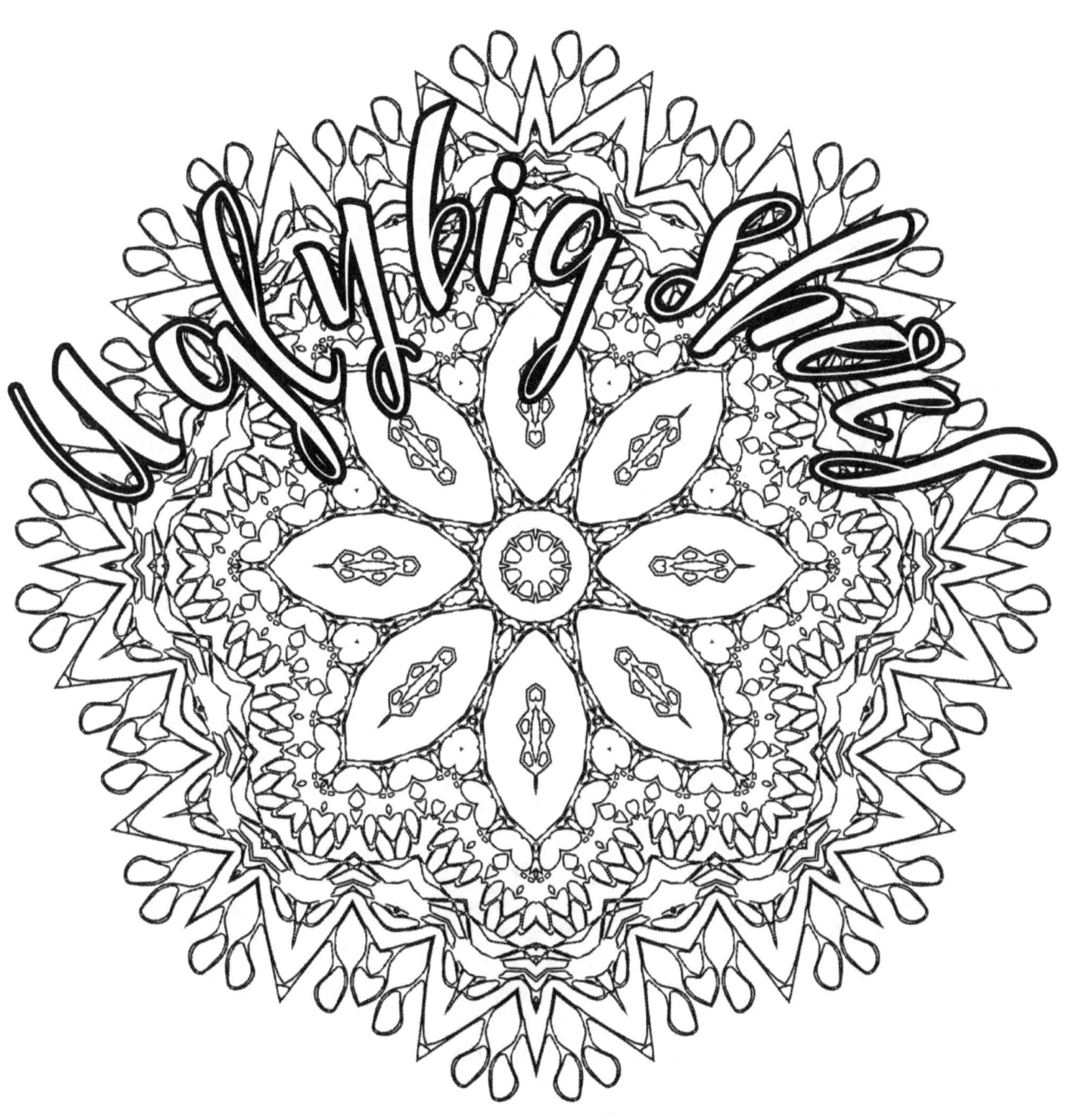

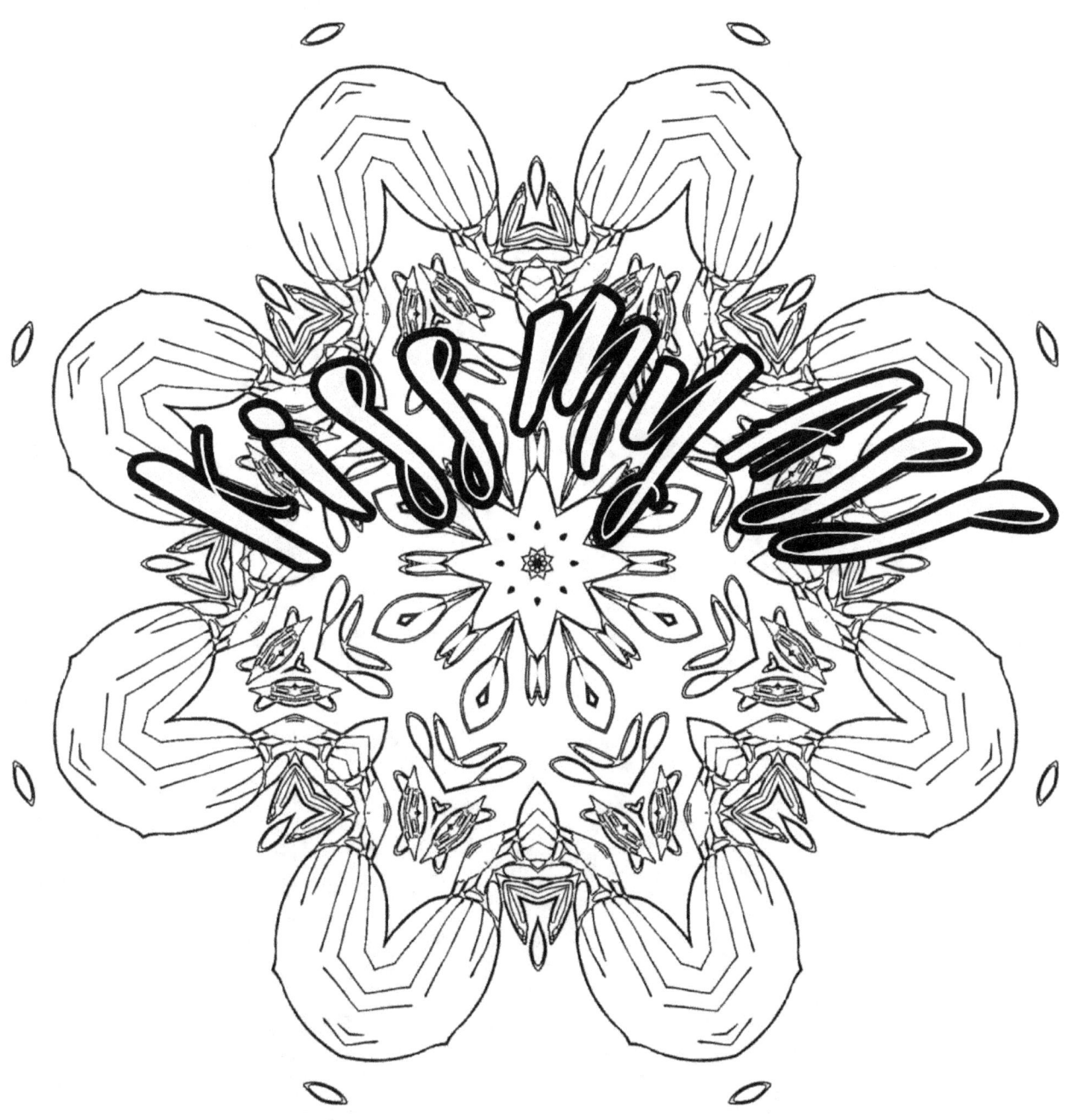

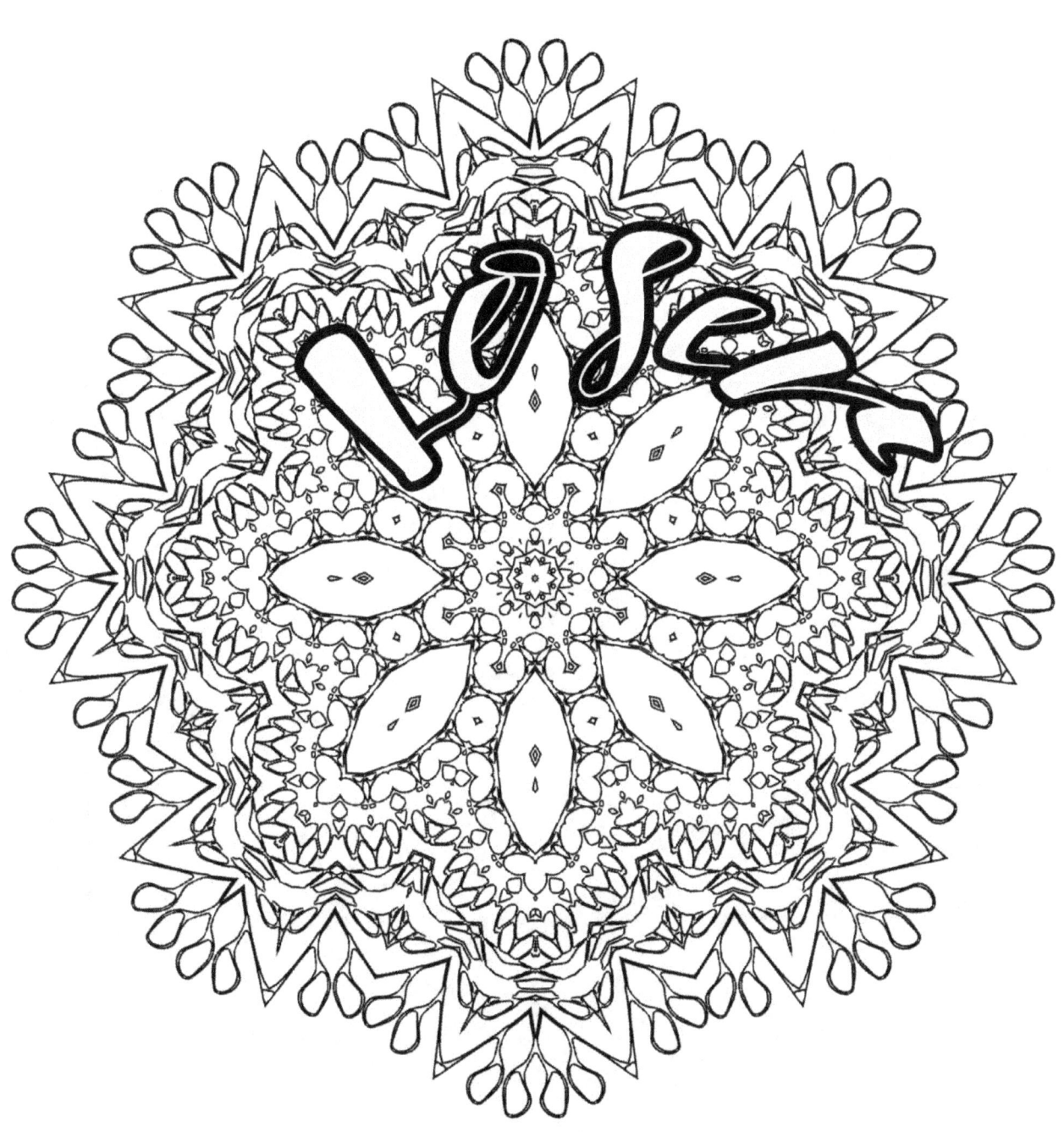

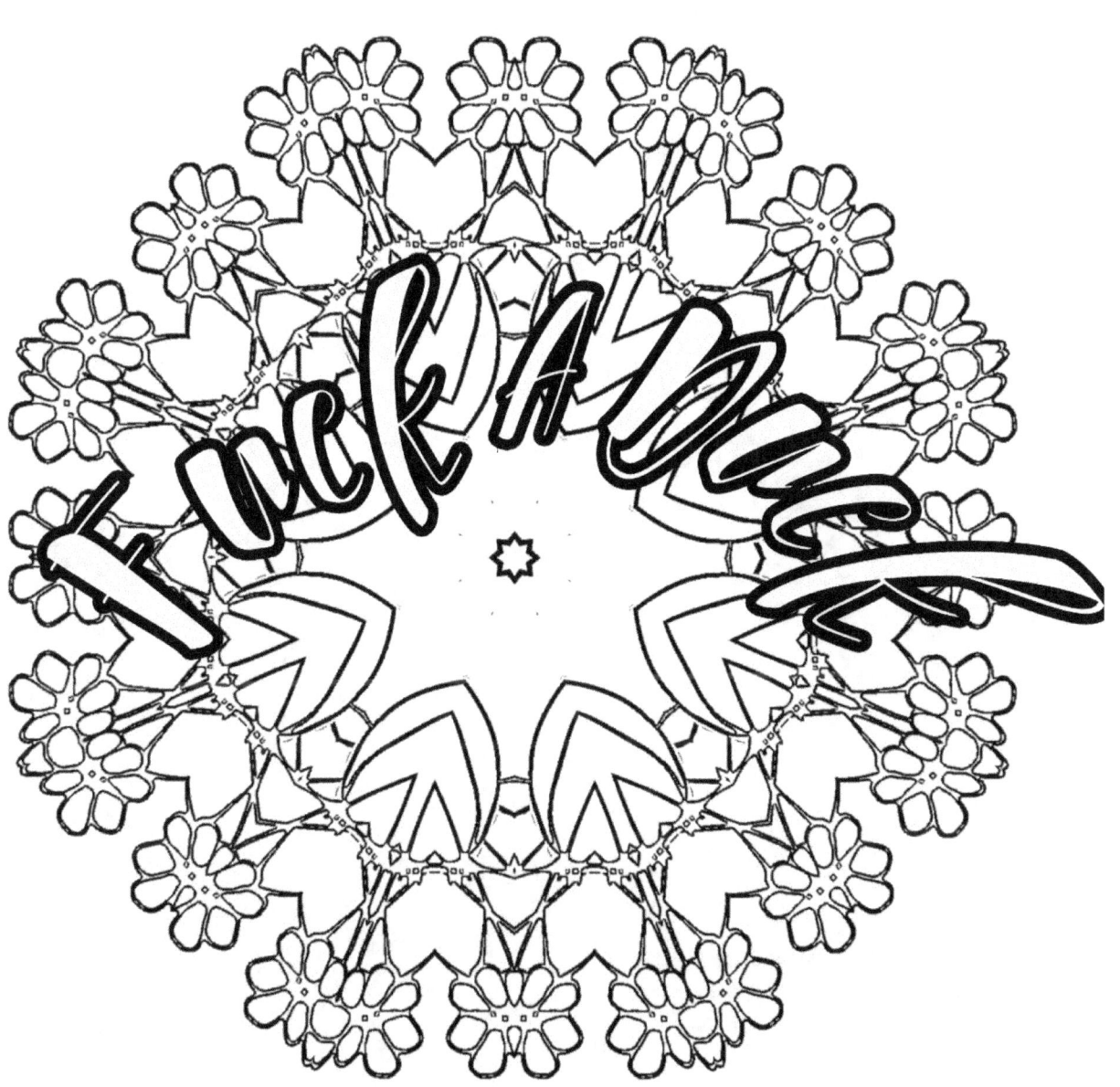

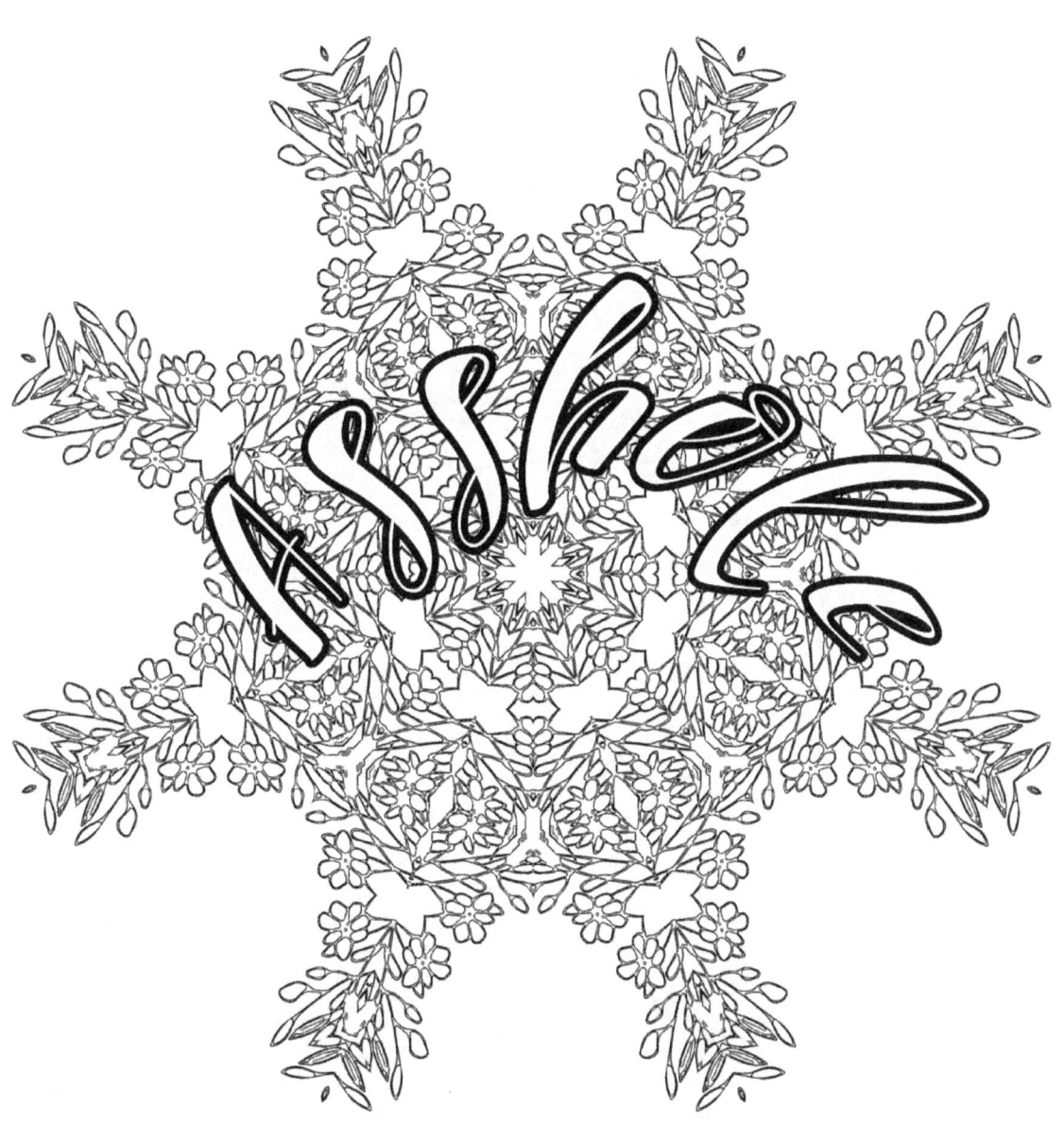

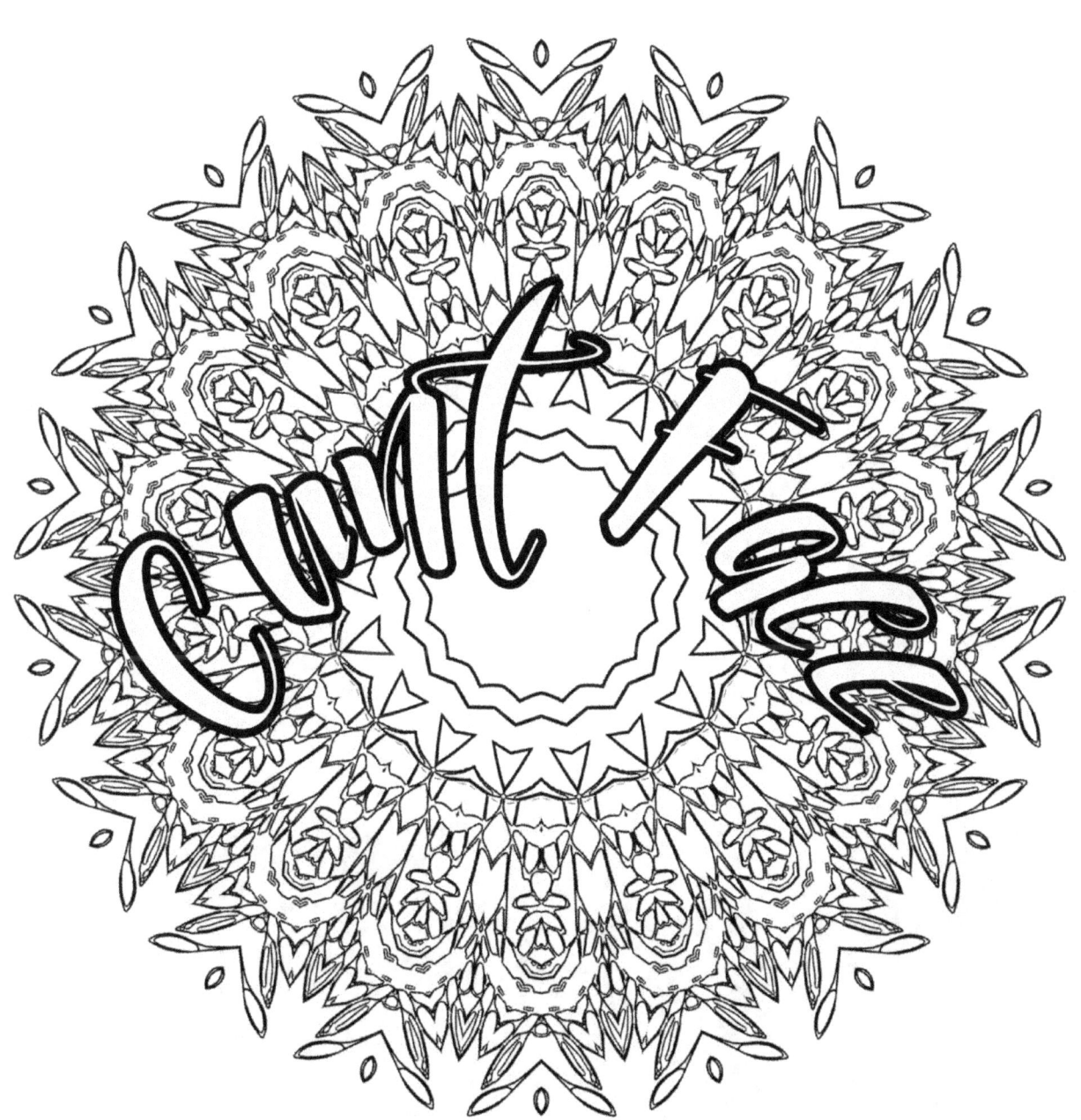

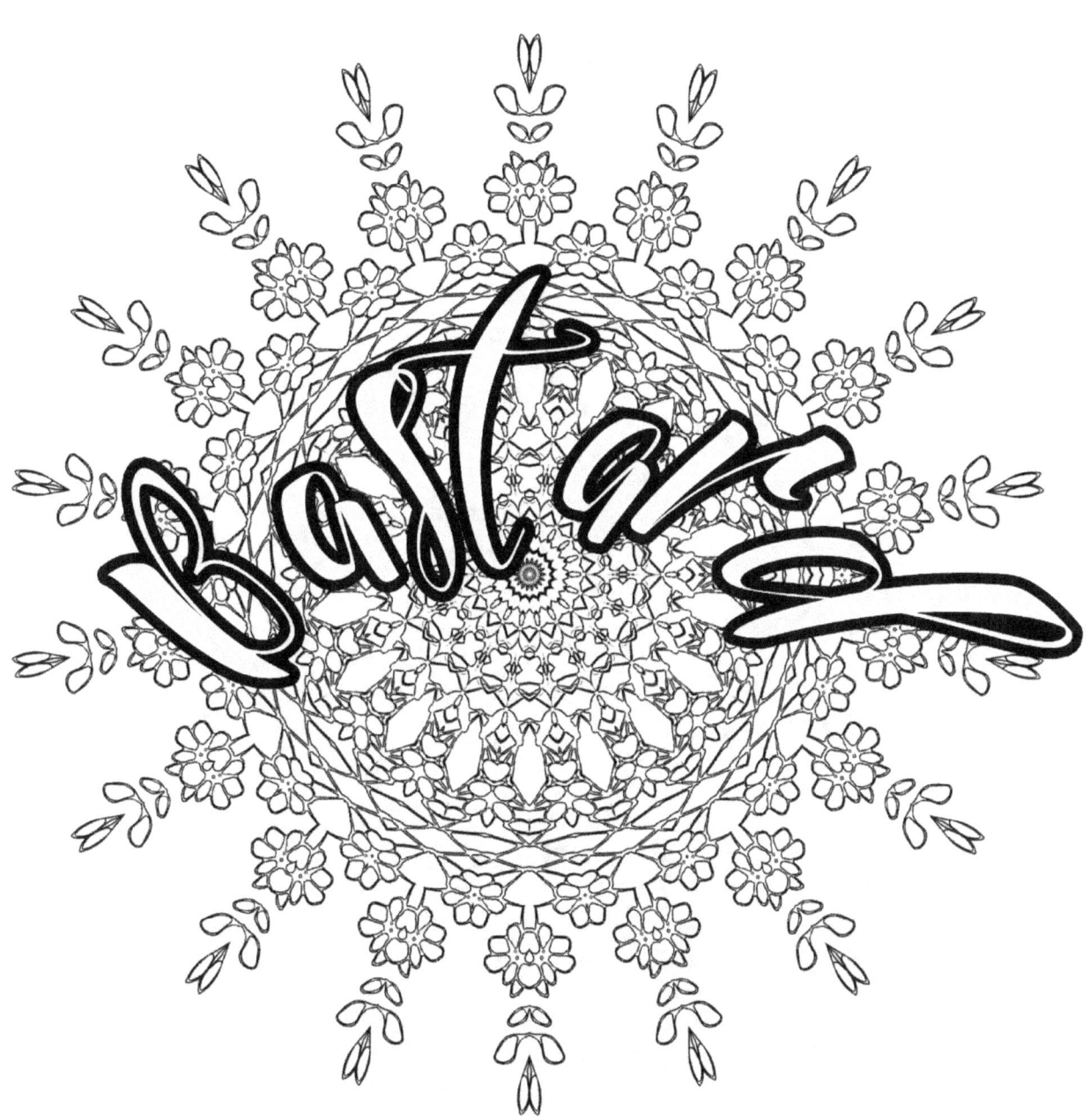

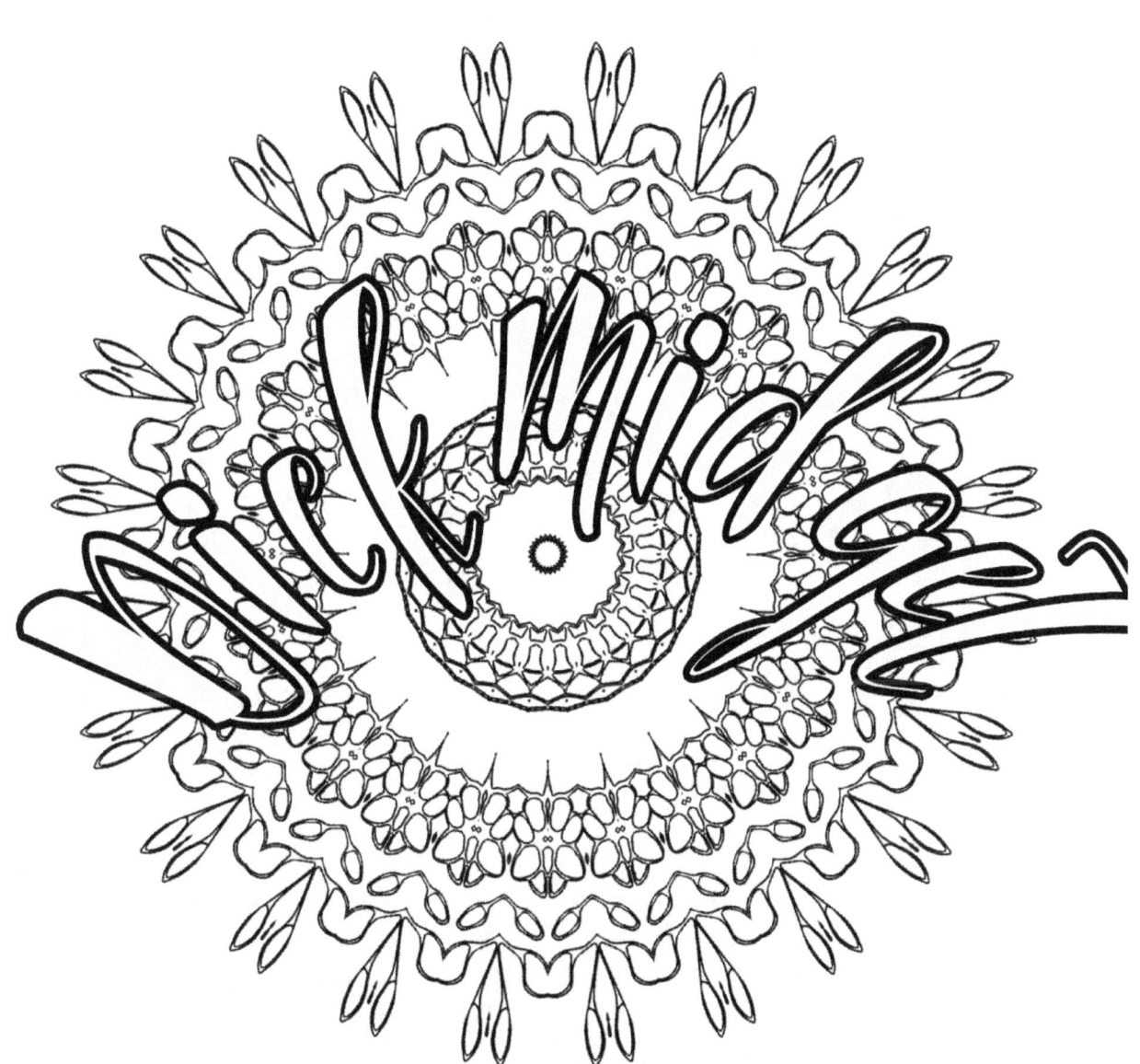

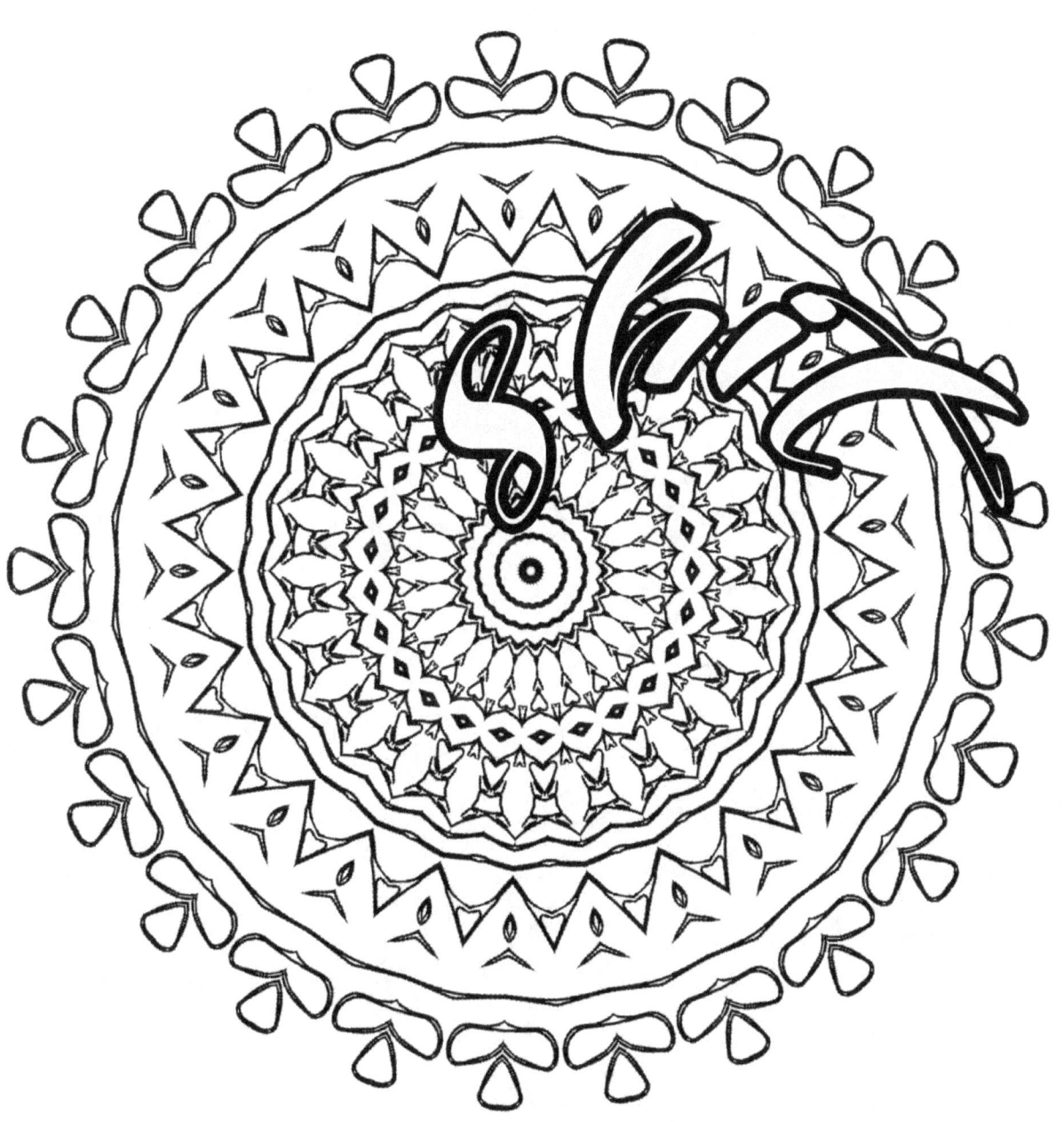

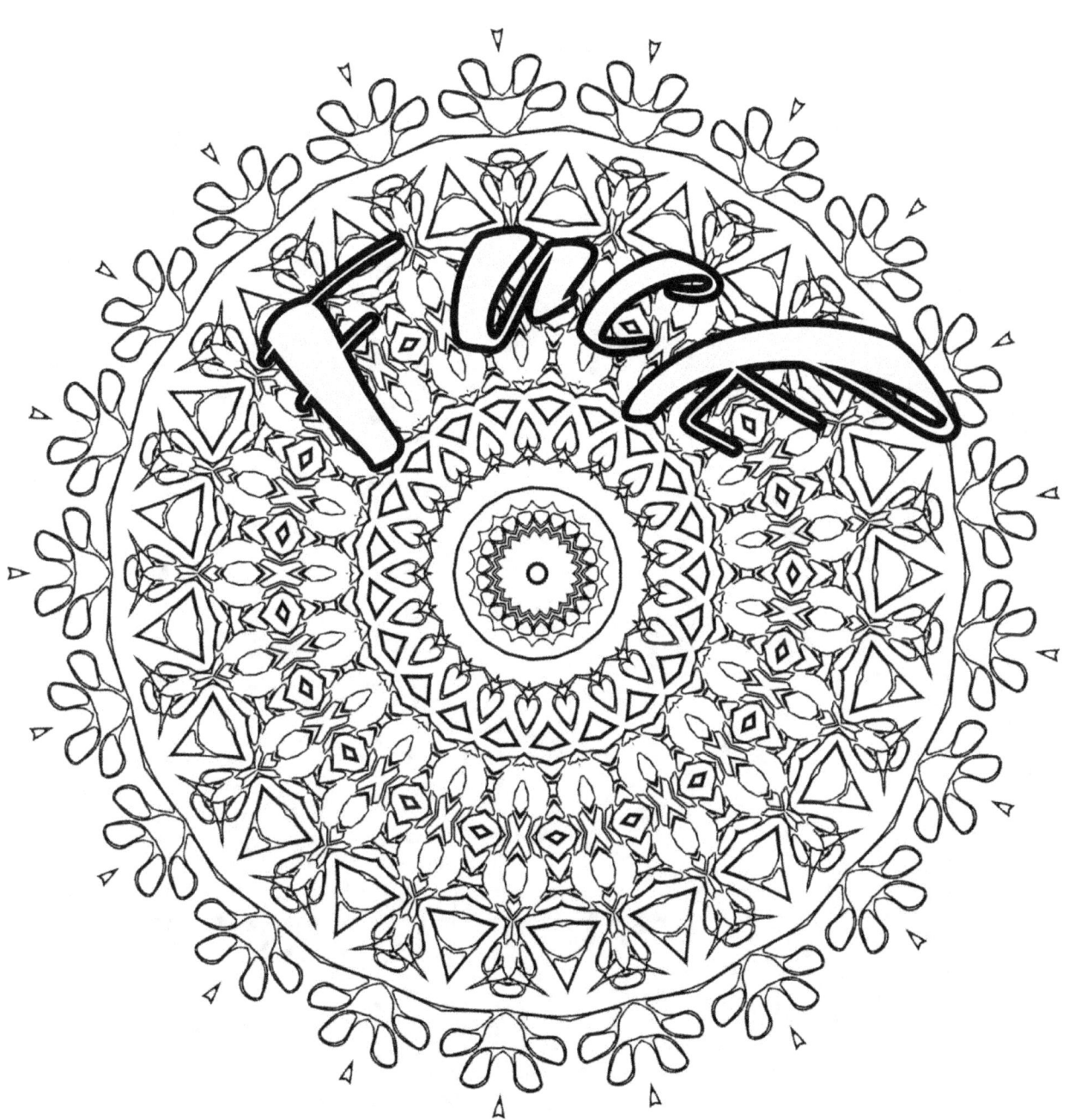

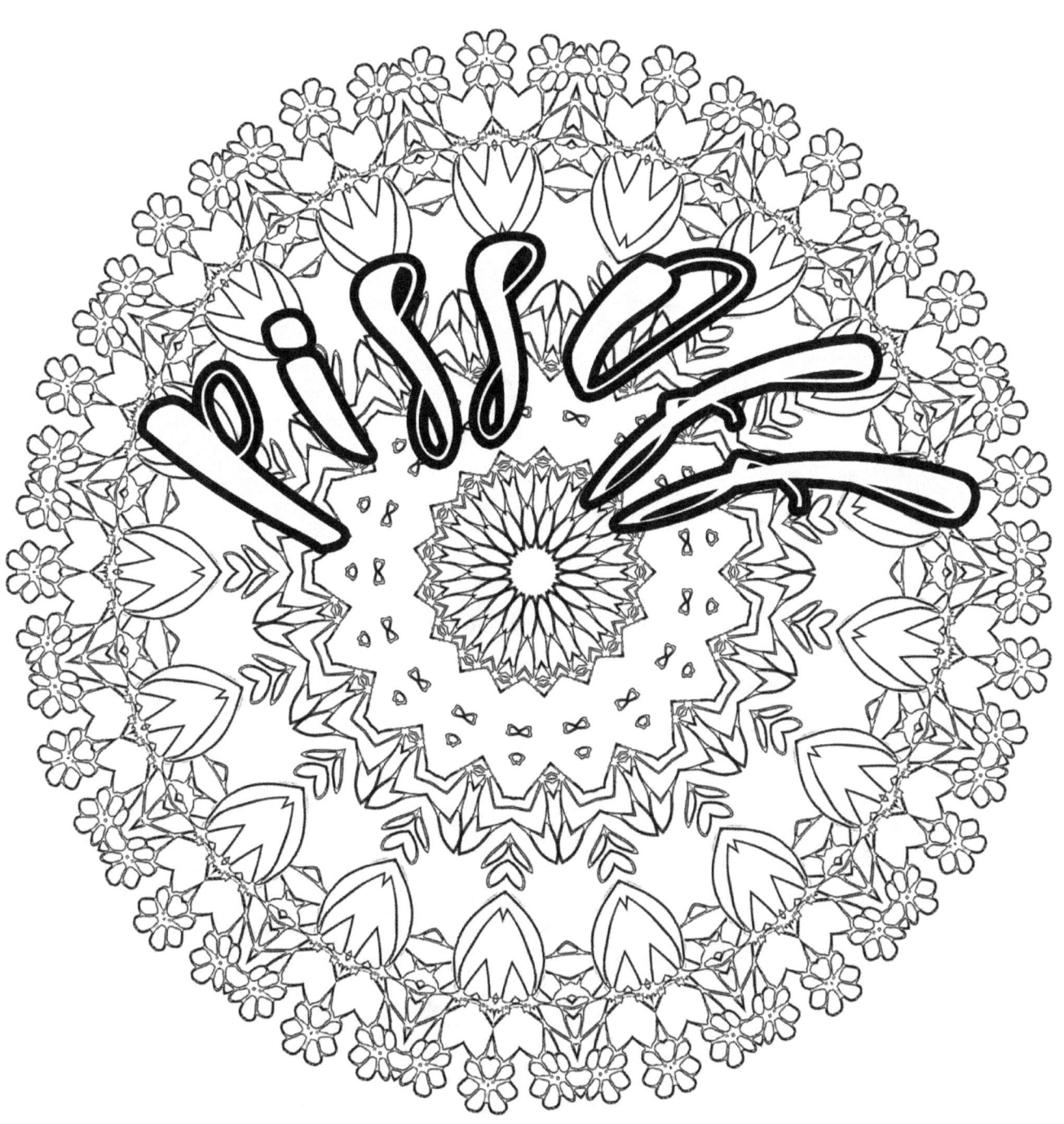

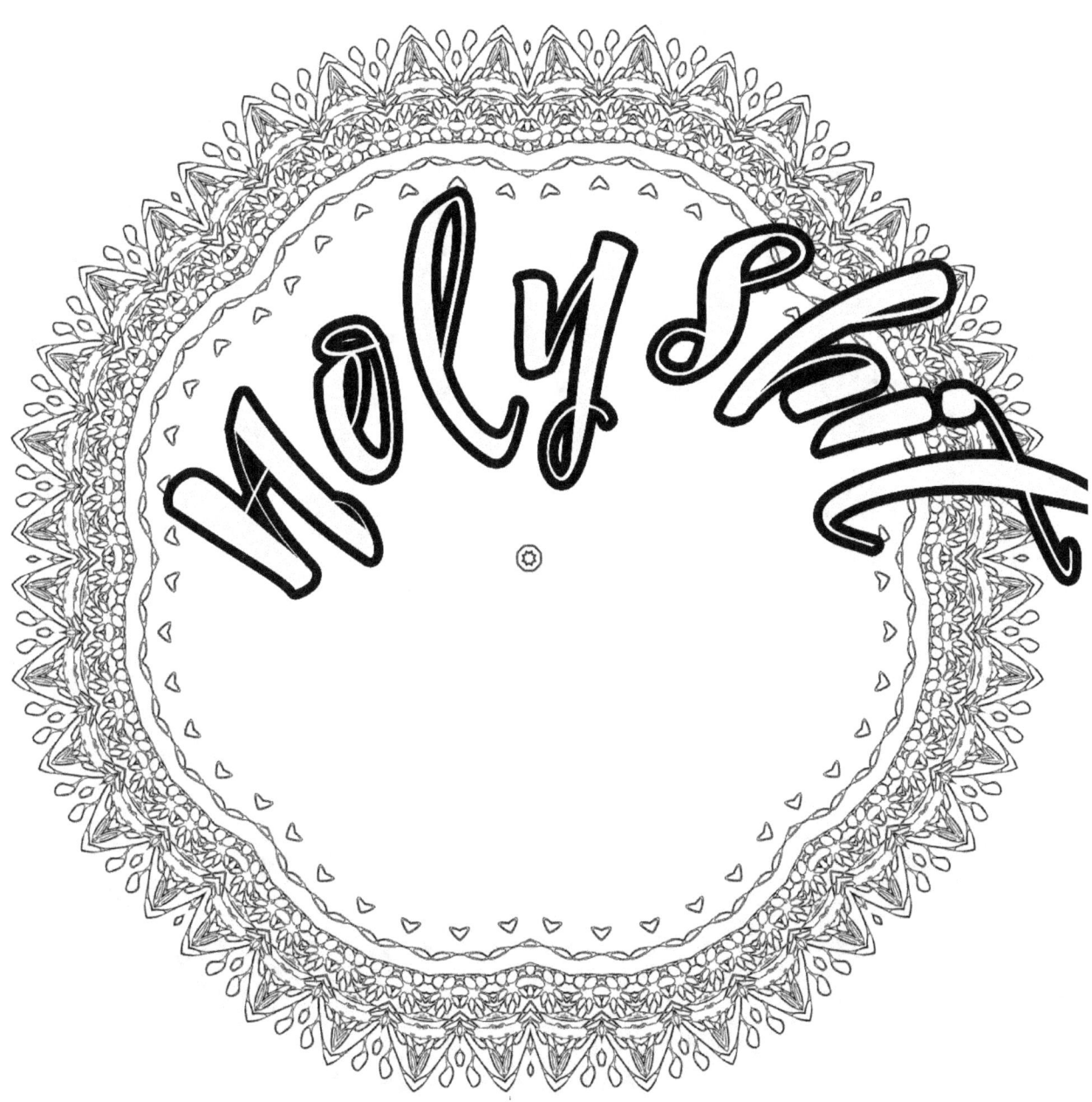

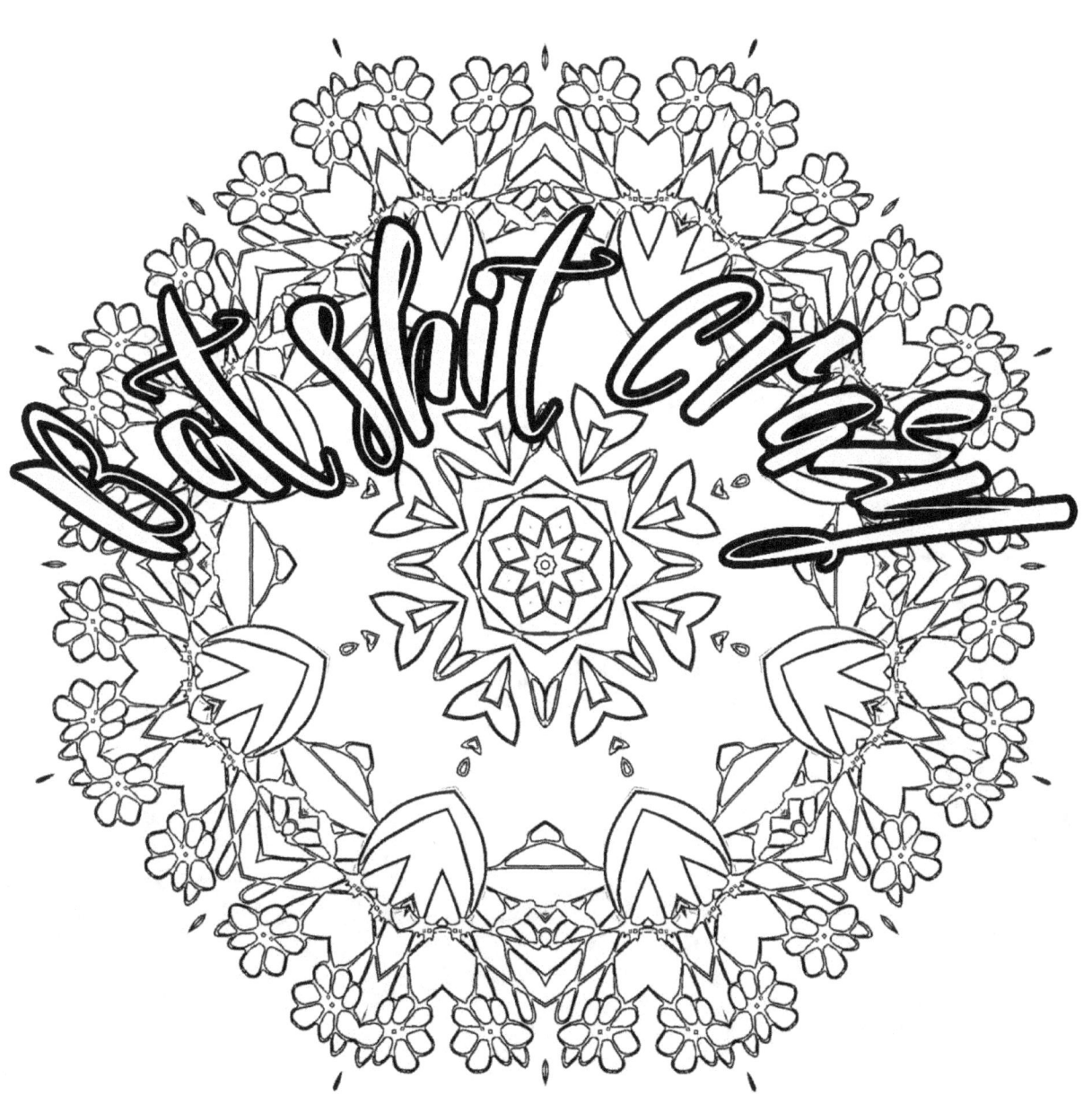

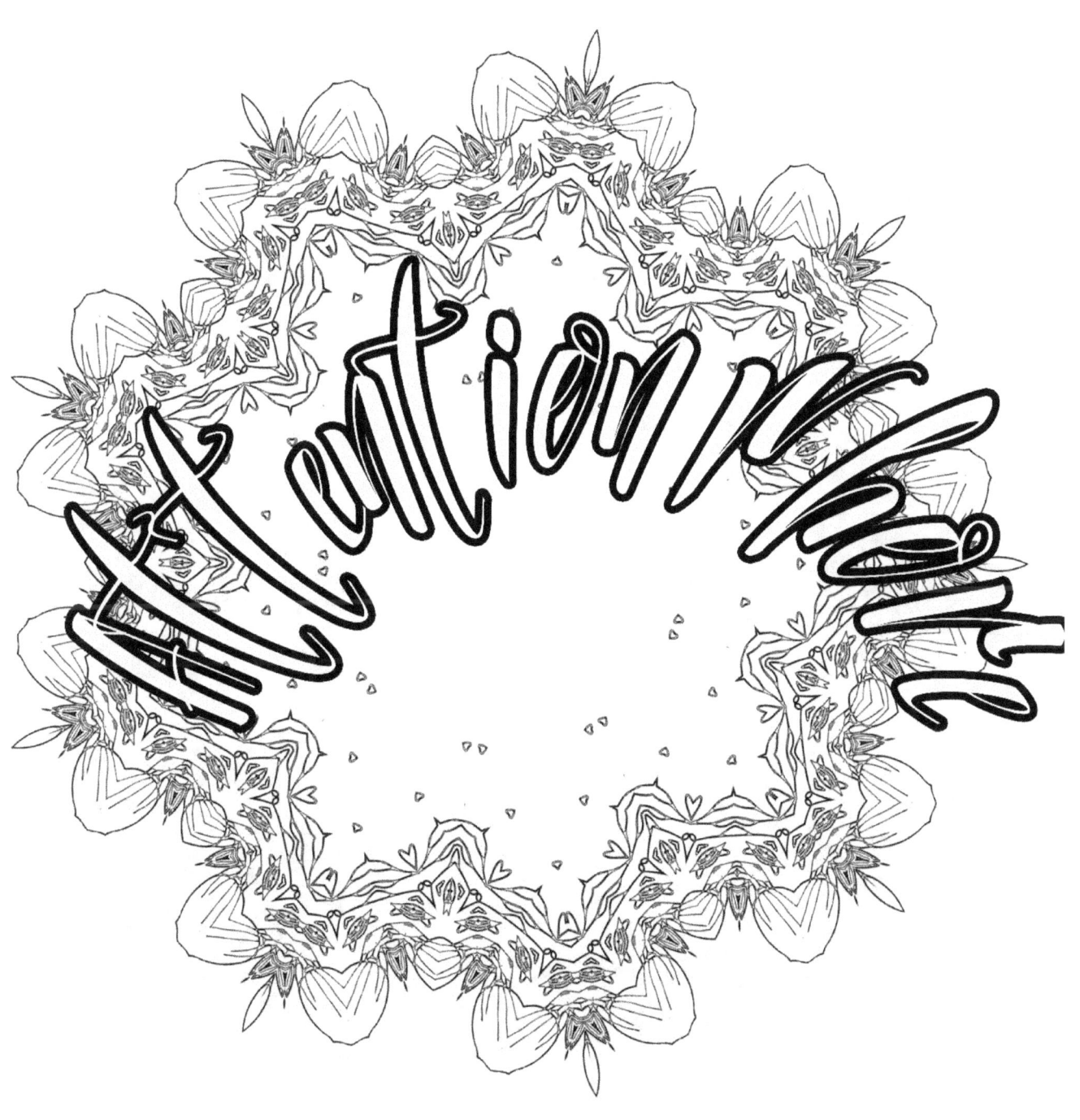

www.ingramcontent.com/pod-product-compliance
Lightning Source LLC
Chambersburg PA
CBHW081750170526
45167CB00009B/3990